When Angels Smile

Songs Of Praise

Inspired Writings
By
Sandra J Yearman

SERAPHIM PUBLISHING LLC

WE WILL BRING LIGHT TO ALL THE DARK PLACES

Registered trademark-
Sandra J Yearman
Seraphim Publishing
438 Water St. Cambridge, WI 53523

Copyright © 2009 Sandra J Yearman
Produced in the United States of America
Author : Sandra J Yearman
Editor: Sandra J Yearman
Cover Design by Sandra J Yearman
Layout and design by Sandra J Yearman

All rights reserved. No part of this book may be reproduced, stored in or introduced into a retrieval system, or transmitted, in any form or by any means, electronic or mechanical, including photocopying or recording or otherwise copied for public or private use—other than for "fair use" as brief quotations embodied in articles and reviews—without written permission from the author.
Library of Congress Control Number: 2009914155

ISBN: 978-0-9841506-4-9

First Edition

Sunshine Sent From Heaven
Stars Across The Miles
Radiance Incomprehensible
When The Angels Smile
Amen
Amen
Amen

CONTENTS

Angels Smile..7
Grateful That I Am...9
Angels And Stars...12
What Color..14
Oh, My Friend..16
The Song Of Forgiveness................................18
A Cry Rang...20
Listen To The Angels Sing.............................22
Inspiration...24
Jesus Our King..26
God Bless My Babies......................................28
The Voice Of Heaven.....................................30
The Angel Whispered.....................................32
When Heaven Smiles......................................34
The Words The Angels Speak........................36
Through Eternity..39
The Crown 41
Listen To Him Calling...................................43
Healer..45
The Sweetness Of The Song..........................48

Gus's Song..50
A Star..52
An Angel With A Lamb.............................54
Precious In My Sight..................................56
The Words Come.......................................58
Tiniest Of Flames.......................................60
If You Could Ask For A Miracle..............62
His Offspring..66
Follow Me...68
A Thanksgiving Prayer...............................70
Radiance..72
He Gives Us Wings....................................74
The Journey 76
I Will Not Leave You.................................79

Dedication

Angels Smile

Angels smile in Heaven
At Love that creatures share
At the Holiness of innocence
At the willingness to care

Angels smile in Heaven
When children remember when
Their Father stood before them
So life would have no end

Angels smile in Heaven
When innocence fore told
When a heart opens without barriers
So the Spirit can take hold

Angels smile in Heaven
When God's children everywhere
Call out to the Father
Speak to Him in prayer

Amen Amen Amen

Grateful That I Am

God I need to ask You
To forgive me for my ways
I get so caught up in life
I forget to thank You every day

This life is so precious
But I did not understand its worth
Until I prayed to Heaven
And the Sword and Cross did girth

Thank You for my blessings
And my darkest days
How would I have learned what I
could conquer
Had not obstacles been in my way

Thank You for the challenges
Thank You for the strife
I learned to make the choices
To gain a better life

Perception was my enemy
Now I see it as a gift
How I view the illusion
I made the Holy shift

Forgive me for not thanking You
Each and every day
I would not have conquered the trail
of tears
I would have lost my way

But even in my darkest moments
You saw me through the tests
You surrounded me with Angels
You held me to Your Breast

Amen Amen Amen

Angels And Stars

Angels and stars
Messengers sent from afar

Love and Grace
God's Presence in this place

The Song of Love
Blessings sent from above

God's Hand
Salvation for man

Acts of Love
Song and dove

Brilliance and fire
The Spirit to inspire

Angels and stars
Messengers sent from afar

Amen Amen Amen

What Color

What is the color of hatred
What is the color of fear
What is the color of bigotry
The demons man calls near

How do you paint a picture
Of mankind as is told
An earth covered in blood
Man's greed painted in gold

How does God show us
Our images in a mirror
When we shriek with horror
And refuse to let Him near

God send Your Light to illuminate
our darkness
Let Your True canvas appear
What is the color of Love
God Bring the Heavens near

Amen Amen Amen

Oh, My Friend

Love unconditional
Joy divine
Another Spirit such as his
In this world I would not find

Ashes from the fire
A star in the darkest night
Embodied Grace and Radiance
To honor as I might

God sends blessings into this world
As answers and as gifts
To help us conquer the darkness
To rise above the rift

A star and yet an anchor
To soar and yet to ground
A friend in life and spirit
Is the Holy gift I found

Amen Amen Amen

The Song Of Forgiveness

The Song of forgiveness
The healing of pain
The Blessings from Heaven
Everything to gain

The Light in the darkness
That reminds us of Love
That heals and makes whole
Sent from above

Forgiveness heals all
Not just the one to whom it was meant
It heals the wounds
In the one from which it was sent

And when we forgive
With the heart of a child
God's Love is complete
And the Angels do smile

Amen Amen Amen

A Cry Rang

A cry rang from the manager
The Angels bowed with Grace
A Song so sweet and pure
Never before heard in such a place

The stars illuminated the night sky
The wind began to speak
To announce to a world
The Savior they did seek

The life in all creation
The answer to the Call
The Father sent a Gift
To save us one and all

And in that single gesture
The veils that did separate
The children from the Father
Were removed, for our sakes

The Heavens and the known world
Were united by that cry
That rang from a manager
That was sent, from on high

Amen Amen Amen

Listen To The Angels Sing

We listen to the Angels sing
A Song so sweet and pure
A Song that transcends ages
A Song we long to hear

Wings of gold will carry
The messengers with their Song
The music will inspire
The message will correct what is wrong

As we listen to their voices
Would we worlds transcend
On the wings of Holy messengers
Our lives will have no end

As we listen to their voices
Overwhelmed and filled with tears
As our hearts are opened
And the Song brings Heaven near

Amen Amen Amen

Inspiration

Inspiration
The touching of souls

The worlds
Transcend

The boundaries
Unite

The Face of God
On this world shines bright

And when He whispers
The souls sing with Grace

And God's inspiration
Is brought to this place

Amen Amen Amen

Jesus Our King

The King's brief appearance in our world
Changed the course of history
Changed the course of man
His footprints will be seen through eternity

He gave us the answers
To questions we are not worthy to ask
He gave us the answers in His life
He showed us the journey Home

He taught us to let go of the ego
He taught us to Love by overcoming our fears
He taught us Forgiveness
He taught us that death is frail

And the Lord God
Spread out His arms
And engulfed all of creation

The King soared
The Word was spoken
The Song poured forth
The Angels sang

Amen Amen Amen

God Bless My Babies

God bless my babies
That they may see
A world from darkness
That is set free

May they enjoy the Love
That God the Father sent
May they know forgiveness
And Grace as it was meant

God bless my babies
That they may see
The Holiness in creation
As created by Thee

May they be warriors
Healers and teachers
Rescuers and ministers
Poets and seekers

May they bless
The earth, where ever they walk
May they speak God's Word
May they teach as taught

God use my home
My house, I pray
To teach the world
Of a better Way

Amen Amen Amen

The Voice Of Heaven

The Voice of Heaven sings tonight
For creatures great and small
A King was born into this world
To save us one and all

And the Grace of Christmas
Blesses from afar
As Heaven's Light unfolds the path
The Light of Heaven's Star

Angels Sing with Glory
Their voices filled with Love
As God sends His Blessings
His Love and Grace from above

And Glory Alleluia
Will the voices ring
As the Promise of Heaven
Our Salvation to bring

Glory, Glory, Glory
Alleluia praises sing
Glory Alleluia
The Voice of Heaven rings

Amen Amen Amen

The Angel Whispered

The Angel whispered softly
His words were filled with Grace
His message was Holy
And brought Healing to the place

Where chaos had become king
Where hatred and fear filled
the beings
Where darkness was exalted
Where life had no meaning

The Song he sang was simple
An ancient Song of life
The words told of the Pathway
To ascend this world of strife

God sends His Angels always
But the world turns them away
A world encased with fear
A world afraid to find a Better Way

Amen Amen Amen

When Heaven Smiles

God fill me with Your Love
Consume me with Your Grace
Let me be Your representative
In the darkness of this place

Help me to sing the Song of Heaven
Help me to sing the Praises of my Lord
Help me to dissolve the darkness
Never let me drop the Sword

Use me as Your Voice
Use me as Your Hand
Help me to bring Your Word
To this world of man

And when my time here has ended
And this body frail and weak
Can no longer sustain me
Return me to the One I seek

Amen Amen Amen

The Words The Angels Speak

Glory, Glory Alleluia
Hear the Angels sing
The Song whispers in the Heavens
The Song that salvation brings

Glory, Glory Alleluia
Let the praises ring
Glory, Glory Alleluia
To our God, The Son, our King

Ancient were the prophets
With God's Words fore told
Of a Savior who would redeem
The lost, the dead, the sold

Glory, Glory Alleluia
Let the praises ring
Glory, Glory Alleluia
To our Savior, Redeemer, our King

The stars will dance in Heaven
The wind will blow on high
The Light that is sent from Heaven
Will destroy the darkest night

Glory, Glory Alleluia
Let the praises ring
Glory, Glory Alleluia
To our Father, our Salvation, Our King

Glory, Glory Alleluia
Blessed be His Name
The Love of Heaven sent
Blessings of the same

Glory, Glory Alleluia
The words the Angels speak

Amen Amen Amen

Through Eternity

Now and through eternity
Let Your Will be done
Lord forgive me

Lord help me to
Walk in Your Path
Throughout this life

No matter what job
What role I play
Let it be with Holiness and Grace

Help me to dissolve
My anger, jealousies and insecurities
And to replace them with Your Holy
Love

Let my life have meaning
Let my presence here have a purpose
Lead me to the places and people You Will

Give me the words and the
Understanding to do Your Will
Lord Bless me
And allow me to Understand the signs and messages
You send to me

Lord this I would ask
Through Eternity...

Amen Amen Amen

The Crown

The crown of thorns they gave Him
They pierced His Holy head
They never understood
The impact of the words they said

The Crown He gained in Glory
When He rose with such Might
Brought the Light of Heaven
To dissolve the hellish night

The Crown He wears with Glory
His Holiness to tell
His Sacrifice for us
His journey into hell

Glory is the Father
Glory is His Might
Glory is His Love
That conquered a world of fright

Amen Amen Amen

Listen To Him Calling

We are all God's children
As drops in the sea
Separate yet One
His Holiness to Be

Our paths may vary
As we take our tests
As we conquer our demons
As we do our best

To find the path where we came from
To find our way Home
To the Father who Loves us
Our souls to Atone

His Voice keeps calling
His Love is Pure
He welcomes His children
His Presence is near

Call out to Your Father
Open your hearts
Listen to Him calling
No more to be apart

Amen Amen Amen

Healer

There was a most remarkable woman
Who walked in God's Holy Light
She cried out to the Heavens
To save God's children from their plight

She emulated Jesus
His teachings and His Ways
She gave Love and Compassion
To God's children all their days

She healed the sick
And blessed the dead
She believed Jesus' words
When He said

We are all God's children
Every creature great and small
He created us
He Loves us one and all

She took those teachings
To streets where others feared to go
She ministered to creatures
That others would not know

She blessed the outcasts
The nameless and the strays
The voiceless and the victims
The ones others threw away

And in her Mercy
Her fame grew
Which helped her in her mission
As others soon knew

She heard the Voice of Jesus
She felt the Hand of God
She was carried by the Spirit
The staff and the rod

Amen Amen Amen

The Sweetness Of The Song

Listen to the Angels sing
Songs of long ago
A Melody through the ages
A Song our souls should know

In the rapture of the chanting
The healing of their Ways
The blessings sent from Heaven
To guard us all our days

Listen to the Angels sing
And know the Song is meant
To lead us to the Father
The Savior that God sent

Floating on the Melody
The sweetness of the Song
The forgiveness from Heaven
To correct the darkest wrong

Amen Amen Amen

Gus's Song

A song of gratitude
A song of thanks and praise
A song he sang to Heaven
Until his end of days

For God saved him from a horror
A broken heart can bring
God saved his life, more than once
And taught him how to sing

Angels bring us always
To the places that we must be
God sends His Angels to us
To help our eyes to see

Some lives enter this world
To learn and some to teach
Some stumble, some fall
And some to Heaven reach

A song he sang of gratitude
For the blessings he received
For the Angels and the Song
For the Love that he believed

Amen Amen Amen

A Star

A friend she has in Heaven
That led her to her home
Where she could trust and love
No more in darkness and pain to roam

The name her mother gave her
Was that of a queen of old
Who stood for love and honor
Her integrity could not be sold

And true she is to her namesake
And true she is to her friend
The love she brings to this world
Is boundless, without end

A Light she brings to the darkness
A pearl on Heaven's chain
She dispels the fears of others
She reminds them of He who reigns

Amen Amen Amen

An Angel With A Lamb

An Angel with a lamb
The Great I AM

Compassion in the stars
Love sent from afar

Fill us with Your Grace
Stand before us in this place

Save us with Your Hand
Every woman, child and man

Angel with creation
Sent to save all the nations

Redeemer walk among us
In You we have trust

Leader of the nations
Author of creation

Love sent from the stars
God is never far

An Angel with a lamb
The Great I AM

Amen Amen Amen

Precious In My Sight

They are precious in my sight
The creatures with which I have
been blessed
The forgotten, the tortured
Those who have failed the Holy tests

Precious are Your children
Your creatures, Your gifts
To teach us of Love
To conquer the rift

Precious is the Love
That You send from above
To teach us to honor
The Sword and the Dove

Precious are the bundles
With which You Grace my door
I promise to heal
I know I can do more

Fill me with honor
Fill me with Grace
Bless me that I may
Bring Your Love to this place

Amen Amen Amen

The Words Come

The words came to him
The music in its right
The mission was
To bring God's Spirit to the night

The words came to him
The music in its right
The mission was
To teach God's children to conquer
the night

The words came to him
The lyrics of the Song
The mission was
To teach God's children to correct
what is wrong

When the mission ended
And the Light was in place
The Angels came for him
And blessed him with God's Grace

Amen Amen Amen

Tiniest Of Flames

Lord in Heaven
Hear me I pray
That the Holiest of Spirits
Consumes us this day

Fill us with Radiance
Purity and Flame
Change our lives
Let nothing remain the same

Let the Holiest of Spirits
Break through the dark walls
And bring Your Holy Light
To these unhallowed halls

Lift us from darkness
Consume us with Grace
Save and Protect us
From the horror of this place

And the tiniest of flames
Will consume the night
Walking with God
Mercy and Might

Amen Amen Amen

If You Could Ask For A Miracle

The child in her innocence
Knelt down to pray
God I have a strange request
That I would like to ask You this day

In Church the preacher asked us
If you could have a miracle, what would you say
I've been thinking about my answer
And now I am ready to pray

I thought of all the things I wanted
I remembered a world in need
I thought of asking for power
I thought of asking for good deeds

I remembered all the prayers I've said
Asking You to help Your children
To feed them and to heal them
To let them know You as a friend

I thought of asking for money
So I could give to every charity
So I could build a church
So I could help them see

But the more I pondered
The answer was plan to see
God if I could ask for a miracle
I would ask that You would walk with me

That You would walk among Your Children
That Your Presence would be felt here
That the lost and hopeless
Would know that Angels are near

Because God, If You would answer this simple prayer
The world itself would change
The Holiness of Your Presence
Our lives would rearrange

Your Light would dissolve the darkness
Your Love would heal this world
You would bring us Home
And all the worlds would herald

That the children reunited with their Father
No longer are they lost and alone
Your Love and Grace have saved us
With Your Mercy we are Atoned

Amen Amen Amen

His Offspring

For we are indeed His offspring
The gifts that He made
The life He created
The life that He saved

For we are God's offspring
His likeness we aspire
His Love we seek
His blessings we desire

For we are His offspring
Said the Father to the Son
Yet we fail to honor our heritage
And the blessings from One

If God is our Father
His children we be
Why do we ignore and betray Him
And fail to honor the Holy Three

Should we dedicate a Father's Day
Just meant to honor the Divine
So the lost offspring
His Presence to find

Amen Amen Amen

Follow Me

Follow Me
Jesus said
Let go of the darkness
You have wed

Follow Me
The path I make
To Heaven's door
For your soul's sake

Follow Me
My Blessed child
I will Love you always
I will ease your trials

Follow Me
And seek the Light
Your Home awaits
Salvation from the night

Amen Amen Amen

A Thanksgiving Prayer

Thank You for this feast
That fills this table so
Thank You for Your Grace
That we are Blessed to know

Thank You for Your Love
And the Angels that You send
Thank You for the radiance
That heals the world of men

Thank You for this family
The friends that we do share
Thank You for the answers
And showing us that You care

Thank You for our lives
Thank You for this day
Thank You for the Son Of God
Who showed the Holy Way

Amen Amen Amen

Radiance

Sunshine sent from Heaven
Stars across the miles
Radiance incomprehensible
When the Angels smile

Love beyond all boundaries
Guard us through the trials
Shepherds all around us
When the Angels smile

How do we understand
Eternity complete
Do we recognize
When Angels we do meet

God sends His messengers
To watch us all the while
To protect and to guide us
God's Love makes the Angels smile

Amen Amen Amen

He Gives Us Wings

He gives us wings
And the ability to fly
It is our choice
Whether we take to the skies

He gives us Love
That bounds without end
It is our choice
Whether we accept the gifts that
He sends

He gives us all we need
To live in this life
It is our choice
Whether we ask to be raised above our
strife

Our purpose, our potential
The roles that we play
It is our choice
To strive to bring a better day

Amen Amen Amen

The Journey

I sought God in nature
I sought God in the stars
I sought God
Both near and far

I traveled creation
To hear His Voice
I sought the wisdom of sages
This was my choice

I read books of Holiness
I prayed with my might
Then a Voice I heard
Said, 'My child, you walk in the Light'

It proceeded to tell me
To my surprise
That my journey
Had been my holy guise

For as I sought Him
And called His Name
I conquered my demons
I was freed of my shame

The journey to Him
The steps that I climbed
Raised me from darkness
Helped me transcend time

He was always with me
I just did not see
Since the darkness I created
Was a barrier to Thee

Amen Amen Amen

I Will Not Leave You

I am not going to leave you here
In the darkness of the night
I will stay with you always
And deliver you from your fright

I will be the candle
That shows you Holy Light
I will be the Angel
That protects you from the night

I will be your anchor
I will be your net
I will be your cord
For I AM Heaven sent

I AM the Answer
I AM the Lamb
I AM your Father
I AM Who I AM

Amen Amen Amen

God Sends His Messengers
To Watch Us All The While
To Protect And To Guide Us
God's Love Makes Them Smile
Amen
Amen
Amen

www.ingramcontent.com/pod-product-compliance
Lightning Source LLC
Chambersburg PA
CBHW051712040426
42446CB00008B/837